UNVEILING
TENERIFE

Your Travel Guide to the Island of Eternal Spring

ESSENTIALS EDITION

SPAIN UNVEILED SERIES

Presented by

Discover your journey!

West Agora Int

WEST AGORA INT
Timișoara 2024
www.tailoredtravelguides.com
WEST AGORA INT S.R.L. All Rights Reserved
Copyright © WEST AGORA INT 2024

WIKI

Tenerife: The Enchanting Island of Natural Wonders and Cultural Riches

Tenerife, the largest of Spain's Canary Islands, is a captivating blend of breathtaking natural landscapes, rich cultural heritage, and a vibrant historical tapestry. Situated in the Atlantic Ocean, off the northwest coast of Africa, Tenerife is renowned for its diverse ecosystems, ranging from dramatic volcanic terrain to lush forests and stunning beaches.

The island's natural splendor is epitomized by the Teide National Park, a UNESCO World Heritage Site, which is home to Mount Teide, Spain's highest peak. This majestic volcano and its surrounding landscapes offer a unique geological spectacle, drawing nature enthusiasts and scientists alike. Tenerife's commitment to environmental conservation is evident in its efforts to preserve these natural wonders, balancing ecological integrity with the thriving tourism sector.

Culturally, Tenerife is a melting pot of influences. The ancient Guanches, the island's original inhabitants, have left an indelible mark on its cultural fabric. The Spanish conquest in the 15th century introduced new traditions, resulting in a rich cultural fusion. This blend is celebrated in Tenerife's numerous festivals, with the Carnival of Santa Cruz de Tenerife being a highlight, known for its exuberant parades and vibrant costumes.

Architecturally, Tenerife boasts a mix of historic and modern structures. The capital, Santa Cruz de Tenerife, features landmarks like the futuristic Auditorio de Tenerife, an icon of contemporary design by Santiago Calatrava. The island's artistic heritage is also notable, with figures like surrealist painter Óscar Domínguez contributing to its cultural landscape.

WIKI

Tenerife's gastronomy reflects its cultural diversity, offering a fusion of traditional Spanish flavors with African and Latin American influences. The island's vineyards, particularly in regions like the Orotava Valley, are celebrated for their distinctive wines, enhancing its culinary appeal.

Despite its beauty and allure, Tenerife faces challenges in managing tourism's impact and preserving its natural and cultural assets. Efforts towards sustainable tourism and heritage conservation are key to maintaining the island's unique charm and ecological balance.

Tenerife is more than just a holiday destination; it is a journey through diverse natural landscapes, rich cultural history, and enduring traditions. For those seeking an immersive experience in an island where nature's majesty meets cultural richness, Tenerife offers an unforgettable exploration of life's vibrant tapestry.

CONTENTS

- 1 — GREETINGS AND RECOMMENDATIONS FROM LOCALS
- 3 — PRACTICAL INFORMATION
- 10 — TOP ATTRACTIONS IN TENERIFE
- 22 — HIDDEN GEMS AND LESSER-KNOWN SIGHTS IN TENERIFE
- 31 — PARKS AND GARDENS IN TENERIFE
- 35 — TENERIFE'S CULINARY SCENE
- 40 — SHOPPING IN TENERIFE
- 43 — FAMILY-FRIENDLY ACTIVITIES IN TENERIFE
- 46 — TENERIFE BY NIGHT
- 58 — ART AND CULTURE IN TENERIFE
- 62 — HISTORICAL AND ARCHITECTURAL LANDMARKS IN TENERIFE
- 66 — DAY TRIPS FROM TENERIFE
- 71 — END NOTE

TENERIFE

ISLAND OF ETERNAL SPRING

Tenerife, the largest of Spain's Canary Islands, is a jewel in the Atlantic Ocean. Known for its diverse landscapes, the island boasts sun-drenched beaches, lush forests, dramatic cliffs, and the towering Mount Teide, Spain's highest peak and an active volcano. Tenerife's rich cultural tapestry weaves together elements from its Guanche indigenous roots, Spanish colonial history, and a vibrant, modern European flair. It's a place where nature's grandeur meets human creativity, resulting in a destination brimming with awe-inspiring experiences.

From the buzzing nightlife of Playa de las Américas to the serene beauty of Teide National Park, Tenerife offers a range of experiences for every kind of traveler. The island's unique climate, a blend of subtropical and temperate, creates an environment where extraordinary flora and fauna thrive, and visitors can enjoy outdoor activities year-round. Whether you're looking to relax on a black sand beach, explore historical towns, or embark on an adventure in the rugged Anaga mountains, Tenerife has something to offer.

This guide aims to be your comprehensive companion to exploring Tenerife. We'll delve into everything from the island's top attractions and hidden gems to its culinary delights and vibrant night scene. Each section is crafted with care, providing detailed descriptions, useful tips, and practical information to help you make the most of your journey. Whether you're planning a family holiday, a romantic getaway, or a solo adventure, this guide will help you navigate the wonders of Tenerife, ensuring an unforgettable experience.

GREETINGS AND INSIGHTS FROM LOCALS

¡Bienvenido, dear traveler! Welcome to Tenerife, the enchanting island of eternal spring, where the azure waves of the Atlantic kiss golden shores and the majestic Teide stands sentinel. As a Tinerfeño, I've basked in the sun-drenched beaches and wandered through the lush, mysterious forests, and I am eager to guide you through the hidden gems and exhilarating experiences that only a true local would know.

Embark on your Tenerife adventure by embracing our island spirit. A warm "hola" and a sunny smile will open doors to unique experiences as you explore this volcanic paradise, from the bustling streets of Santa Cruz to the serene hamlets perched in the Anaga Mountains.

You might be captivated by the allure of the Teide National Park. Here, the landscape transforms from verdant forests to lunar-like terrain, with the mighty Teide volcano reigning over the island. This natural wonderland is a testament to Tenerife's vibrant geology, offering trails that lead to breathtaking vistas and hidden craters.

For a brush with our cultural tapestry, meander through the historic town of La Laguna. This UNESCO World Heritage Site, with its beautifully preserved colonial architecture and vibrant student life, provides a glimpse into Tenerife's rich history and youthful energy.

When the island flavors beckon, venture to a local guachinche. These family-run eateries offer authentic Canarian cuisine – from succulent "papas arrugadas" with "mojo picón" to fresh "pescado del día". Remember, here in Tenerife, dining is a celebration of land and sea, infused with the joy of island life.

As twilight unfurls its beauty, the beaches of Costa Adeje offer a tranquil retreat. The whisper of the ocean waves, under a canopy of stars, creates a magical ambiance, perfect for a serene evening stroll or a reflective moment by the sea.

In the heart of Tenerife, the charming town of Masca awaits. Nestled in the Teno Mountains, its winding roads and picturesque vistas are like stepping into a storybook, a hidden escape from the more frequented tourist paths.

Tenerife's essence is its mesmerizing blend of natural wonders, cultural richness, and the warm-heartedness of its people. We, the Tinerfeños, are here with open arms, ready to share the magic of our beloved island with you. ¡Hasta pronto, dear traveler, and may your journey through Tenerife be filled with the spirit of adventure and the warmth of the Canarian sun!

PRACTICAL INFORMATION

Currency The currency in Tenerife is the Euro (€). Credit cards are widely accepted, and ATMs are readily available, but it's a good idea to carry some cash for smaller transactions, especially in remote areas.

Transportation Tenerife has two airports: Tenerife North (Los Rodeos) and Tenerife South (Reina Sofia). The island's public transportation system includes buses (guaguas) and taxis. Buses are an economical way to travel, with extensive routes covering most of the island. Taxis are readily available and metered, offering a more convenient but pricier option.

Driving in Tenerife Renting a car is a great way to explore Tenerife, especially its more remote areas. Remember to drive on the right side of the road. Roads can be steep and winding, especially in mountainous regions, so be cautious.

Climate Tenerife enjoys a mild, subtropical climate year-round. The south is typically warmer and drier than the north. Summer temperatures average around 28°C (82°F), while winter temperatures hover around 20°C (68°F). The mountain areas can be cooler, so packing layers is advisable.

PRACTICAL INFORMATION

Language

Spanish is the official language. English is widely spoken in tourist areas, but learning a few basic Spanish phrases can enhance your experience, especially in less touristy areas.

Power sockets and adapters

Sockets and Adapters: Tenerife uses Type C and F power sockets, typical in Europe. The standard voltage is 230V. Travelers from outside Europe will likely need an adapter.

Shopping

Tenerife offers a range of shopping experiences, from modern malls and designer boutiques to traditional markets selling local crafts and produce. Shops typically open from 9:00 AM to 1:00 PM and 4:00 PM to 8:00 PM, with some variations.

Tipping

Tipping in Tenerife is appreciated but not obligatory. In restaurants, rounding up the bill or leaving a 5-10% tip is customary for good service. For taxi drivers, rounding up to the nearest euro is common.

PRACTICAL INFORMATION

USEFUL LINKS AND PHONE NUMBERS

Emergency Services

All Emergencies: 112 (Police, Fire Brigade, Ambulance)
Local Police (Policía Local): Varies by municipality, but 112 can redirect as needed

Transportation

Tenerife North Airport (Los Rodeos): +34 913 211 000, www.aena.es/en/tenerife-norte-ciudad-de-la-laguna.html
Tenerife South Airport (Reina Sofía): +34 913 211 000, www.aena.es/en/tenerife-sur.html
Titsa Buses: +34 922 531 300, www.titsa.com/index.php/en/ (for bus routes and schedules across the island

Tourist Information

Canary Islands Tourism: www.hellocanaryislands.com
Tenerife Tourist Information Offices: www.webtenerife.com
Santa Cruz Tourist Office www.elcorazondetenerife.com

Hospitals

Hospital Universitario Nuestra Señora de Candelaria (Santa Cruz): +34 922 602 000
www.gobiernodecanarias.org/sanidad/scs/hospitaldelacandelaria
Canary Islands Health Information - https://www3.gobiernodecanarias.org/sanidad/scs

Local Government

Tenerife Local Administration: www.tenerife.es
Canary Islands local Government: www.gobiernodecanarias.org

Maps

For print versions - quick acces through QR codes after the End Note

Tenerife maps:
www.ontheworldmap.com/spain/islands/tenerife/
Tenerife Tourist Map:
www.ontheworldmap.com/spain/islands/tenerife/tenerife-tourist-map.jpg
Tenerife Road Map:
www.ontheworldmap.com/spain/islands/tenerife/tenerife-road-map.jpg
Tenerife Bus Map:
www.ontheworldmap.com/spain/islands/tenerife/tenerife-bus-map.jpg
Tenerife Resorts and Beaches:
www.ontheworldmap.com/spain/islands/tenerife/tenerife-resorts-and-beaches-map.jpg

PRACTICAL INFORMATION
TENERIFE GENERAL MAP

Free high resolution & download at: https://osm.org/go/bkqsps Copyright @ OpenStreetMaps

PRACTICAL INFORMATION
TENERIFE GENERAL MAP

Free high resolution & download at: https://osm.org/go/bkqsps Copyright @ OpenStreetMaps

SANTA CRUZ DE TENERIFE MAP

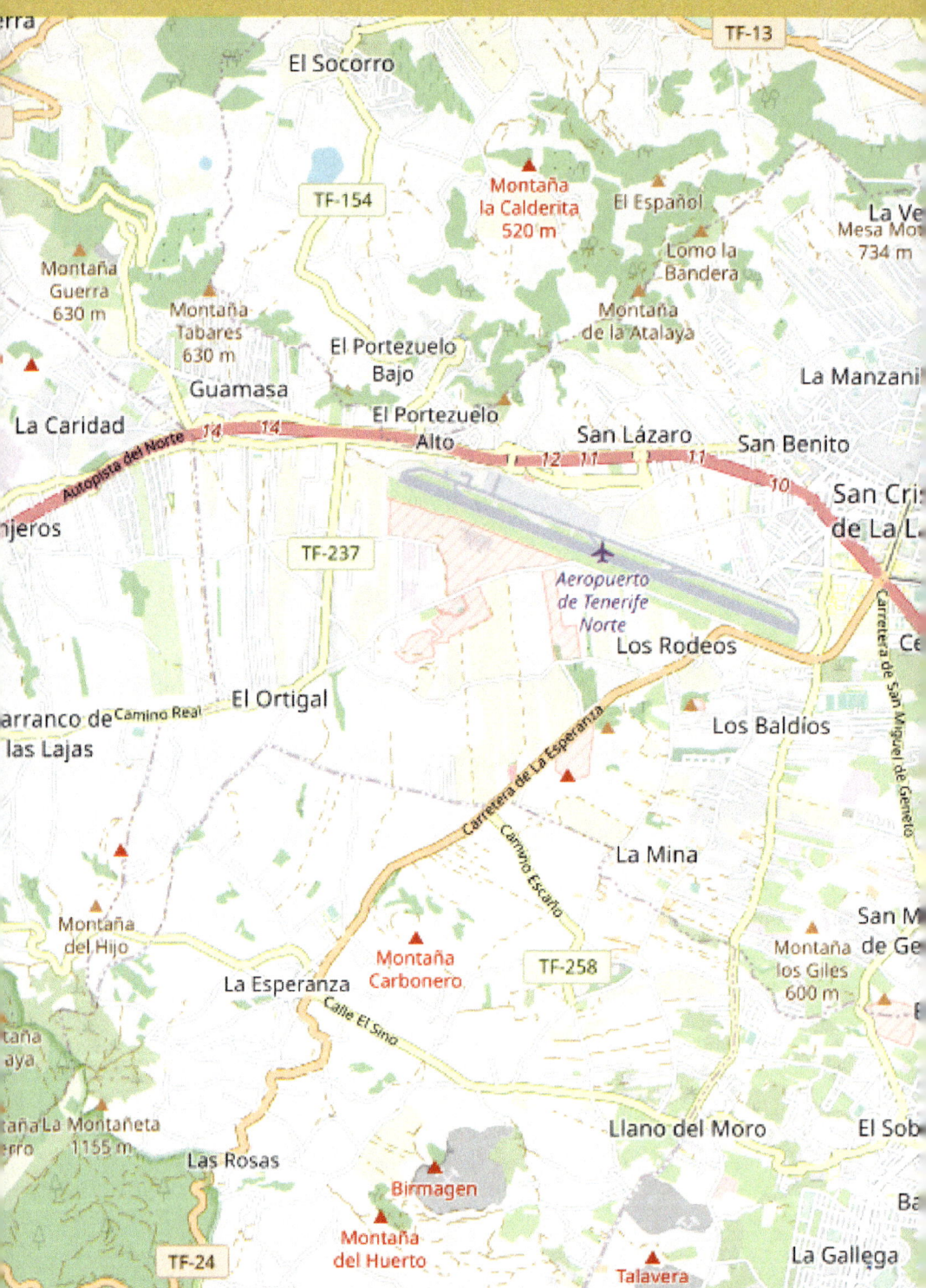

Free high resolution & download at: https://osm.org/go/bmA9WkL Copyright @ OpenStreetMaps

SANTA CRUZ DE TENERIFE MAP

TOP ATTRACTIONS IN TENERIFE
TEIDE NATIONAL PARK

Teide National Park, a UNESCO World Heritage Site in Tenerife, is an extraordinary destination for nature enthusiasts and adventurers alike. The park is renowned for Mount Teide, Spain's highest peak and a dormant volcano, which creates a mesmerizing backdrop. This natural paradise offers a unique, lunar-like landscape filled with craters, ancient rivers of petrified lava, and an array of endemic flora and fauna, making it a haven for biodiversity.

Visitors to the park can immerse themselves in its beauty through various activities. Hiking enthusiasts will find a network of trails that navigate through the rugged terrain, offering both challenging and leisurely routes suitable for all levels. For those who wish to witness the grandeur of Mount Teide without the trek, a cable car ride provides an effortless ascent, presenting awe-inspiring panoramic views from near the summit.

Tip: Experience the park's magic under the starlit sky by booking a guided night tour. Teide National Park is one of the world's best stargazing spots, offering a clear, unobstructed view of the cosmos that is truly unforgettable.

Location: Central Tenerife
Website: www.volcanoteide.com/en

SIAM PARK

Siam Park, situated in the heart of Tenerife, is an extraordinary water park that transports its visitors to a Thai-inspired paradise. Known as one of the best water parks globally, it offers an array of thrilling water slides, each uniquely designed to deliver an adrenaline rush. The park's star attraction, the wave pool, is renowned for generating some of the largest artificial waves in the world, providing an unparalleled surfing experience.

The park caters to all ages, featuring attractions ranging from high-speed slides for thrill-seekers to a leisurely lazy river that meanders through its lush, tropical landscape. Siam Park's dedication to an authentic Thai ambiance is evident in its meticulous architecture and landscaping, creating an immersive and exotic atmosphere.

Tip: To maximize your experience, consider purchasing a fast pass. This allows you to bypass the queues on the most popular rides, ensuring more time for enjoyment. Additionally, don't miss the opportunity to try surfing in the wave pool - a unique experience that adds to the park's appeal.

Location: Av. Siam, s/n, 38660 Costa Adeje, Santa Cruz de Tenerife, Spain

Website: www.siampark.net

LORO PARQUE

Loro Parque, nestled in Tenerife, has grown from its origins as a parrot park to become one of the world's premier zoological gardens. This esteemed park is renowned for its commitment to animal welfare and conservation, setting a standard in the zoological community. It houses an impressive diversity of animals, ranging from the majestic tigers and gentle gorillas to the delicate jellyfish. A key highlight is the world's largest indoor penguin exhibition, a marvel that replicates the Antarctic environment, offering a glimpse into the lives of these charming birds.

The park also features spectacular shows, with the Orca Ocean show and the playful sea lion performances being visitor favorites. These shows not only entertain but also educate audiences about the animals and the importance of conservation efforts.

Tip: Upon arrival, check the show schedules to effectively plan your day. To deepen your experience, consider taking a behind-the-scenes tour. These tours offer a unique perspective on the park's operations and a closer look at the care and dedication behind each exhibit.

Location: Av. Loro Parque, s/n, 38400 Puerto de la Cruz, Santa Cruz de Tenerife, Spain
Website: www.loroparque.com/en/

LOS GIGANTES CLIFFS

The Los Gigantes Cliffs, aptly named 'The Giants', stand as one of Tenerife's most breathtaking natural wonders. These imposing rock walls, rising dramatically from the Atlantic Ocean, reach staggering heights of between 500 to 800 meters, creating a truly magnificent sight. The sheer scale and beauty of these cliffs can be fully appreciated when viewed from the sea, offering a perspective that highlights their grandeur.

Boat tours, readily available from the nearby marina in the quaint town of Los Gigantes, provide the perfect opportunity to experience these natural marvels up close. The town itself adds to the charm of the visit, with its inviting marina, an array of restaurants, and a tranquil atmosphere that contrasts with the towering presence of the cliffs.

Tip: Embarking on a boat trip not only gives you an unrivaled view of the cliffs but also presents the possibility of encountering dolphins and whales in their natural environment, adding an extra layer of excitement to the excursion.

Location: Acantilados de Los Gigantes, Santa Cruz de Tenerife, Spain (coord: 28°15'45.1"N 16°50'32.0"W)
Website: www.hellocanaryislands.com/nature-spaces/tenerife/los-gigantes-cliffs/

MASCA VILLAGE

Masca Village, a hidden gem nestled in the rugged Teno Mountains of Tenerife, offers a glimpse into a bygone era. This quaint hamlet, characterized by its traditional Canarian architecture and serene atmosphere, stands as a stark contrast to the bustling tourist centers elsewhere on the island. The village's picturesque setting is enhanced by breathtaking valley views and terraced landscapes that have been cultivated over centuries.

Masca is not just a visual treat but also a haven for hikers. It serves as the starting point for the renowned Masca Gorge hike, a trail that descends through a spectacular ravine and culminates at a beautiful, secluded beach. This trek is both challenging and rewarding, offering stunning natural scenery and a sense of adventure.

Tip: For those planning to tackle the Masca Gorge hike, it's essential to wear sturdy hiking shoes and carry plenty of water. The trail can be demanding, but the scenic rewards are unparalleled.

Location: C. Lomo del Medio, 38489 Masca, Santa Cruz de Tenerife, Spain
Website: www.hellocanaryislands.com/places-full-of-charm/tenerife/masca/

WHALE & DOLPHIN WATCHING TRIPS

Tenerife, a haven for marine wildlife enthusiasts, offers some of the world's most impressive opportunities for whale and dolphin watching. The island's waters are a natural habitat for a diverse array of marine mammals, including the frequently sighted pilot whales and playful bottlenose dolphins. The chance of encountering these magnificent creatures is high throughout the year, making Tenerife a premier destination for wildlife observation.

From the ports of Los Cristianos, Costa Adeje, and other locations in South Tenerife, numerous tour operators conduct boat trips into the heart of these mammals' natural habitat. These excursions not only provide a chance to witness these animals up close but also offer an educational insight into their behaviors and the ecosystem they inhabit. On rare occasions, visitors might even spot the elusive blue whale, adding to the thrill of the experience.

Tip: When choosing a whale and dolphin watching trip, consider opting for an eco-friendly tour operator. These companies prioritize responsible wildlife watching practices and are actively involved in conservation efforts, ensuring that your experience contributes positively to the preservation of these species.

Location: Boat trips typically depart from ports in South Tenerife
Website: www.webtenerife.co.uk/what-to-do/nature/whale-and-dolphin-watching/

GARACHICO

Garachico, nestled in the northwest of Tenerife, is a town rich in history and adorned with natural beauty. This picturesque locale, once the island's most vital port, has a compelling story of resilience and rebirth. Following a devastating volcanic eruption in 1706, which dramatically altered its landscape and coastline, Garachico was meticulously rebuilt. Today, it stands as a testament to the enduring spirit of its community.

Visitors to Garachico are greeted with a tapestry of charming, well-preserved historical architecture, offering a window into the past. The town's unique feature is its natural rock pools, El Caletón, created by flowing volcanic lava and now a serene spot for swimming and relaxation. Strolling through Garachico's quaint streets, one can sense the tranquil ambiance that pervades this town, making it an ideal destination for those seeking to experience Tenerife's rich history and natural wonders in a more relaxed atmosphere.

Tip: While in Garachico, don't miss the opportunity to take a dip in the natural pools of El Caletón. These pools, with their crystal-clear waters and unique volcanic formations, offer a memorable and invigorating experience.

Location: Northwest Tenerife - C. Eutropio Rodríguez de la Sierra, 2, 38450 Garachico, Santa Cruz de Tenerife, Spain

Website: www.hellocanaryislands.com/places-full-of-charm/tenerife/garachico-old-town/

DRAGON TREE IN ICOD DE LOS VINOS

The Dragon Tree (Dracaena draco) in Icod de los Vinos stands as a living monument and a symbol of Tenerife's natural heritage. Estimated to be around 800 years old, it is revered as one of the oldest and most majestic specimens of its kind. This tree's distinctive appearance, with its wide, umbrella-like canopy and thick, gnarled trunk, makes it a fascinating and photogenic landmark.

Nestled within Parque del Drago, this ancient tree is surrounded by a variety of endemic plant species, offering visitors a unique insight into the diverse flora of the Canary Islands. The park itself is a tranquil space, perfect for leisurely walks and nature observation.

Tip: To enhance your visit, consider exploring the historic town of Icod de los Vinos. Renowned for its local wine production, the town offers a blend of cultural and historical experiences, complementing the natural allure of the Dragon Tree.

Location: P.° Nicolas Estevez Borges, 1, 38430 Icod de los Vinos, Santa Cruz de Tenerife, Spain
Website: www.hellocanaryislands.com/museums-and-places-of-interest/tenerife/millennial-dragon-tree-park/

SAN CRISTOBAL DE LA LAGUNA

San Cristobal de la Laguna, a city resonating with historical and cultural significance, is a UNESCO World Heritage Site located in northeastern Tenerife. This city is celebrated for its beautifully preserved colonial architecture, which has served as an influential model for urban development in many colonial cities across the Americas. Exploring La Laguna is like stepping back in time; its streets are lined with vibrant, colorful buildings that reflect the rich history of the region.

Visitors to La Laguna can explore an array of historic churches, each with its unique architectural and artistic charm. The city is not only a hub of history but also a center of contemporary cultural life. It hosts various cultural events throughout the year, adding to its dynamic atmosphere. Furthermore, as the home to the University of La Laguna, the city is imbued with a youthful, energetic vibe, thanks to its student population.

Tip: Dive into the local culture by visiting the city's markets and cafes, where you can experience everyday life in La Laguna. Don't miss the chance to savor the local cuisine at one of the city's many restaurants, offering authentic Canarian dishes.

Location: Northeast Tenerife, near the Tenerife North Airport San Cristóbal de La Laguna, Tenerife, Spain
Website: www.spain.info/en/destination/san-cristobal-laguna/

ANAGA RURAL PARK

Anaga Rural Park, situated in the northeastern reaches of Tenerife, is a breathtaking expanse of natural beauty. This protected reserve is famed for its dramatic landscapes, encompassing rugged mountains, deep ravines, and dense laurel forests, a vestige of ancient times. It's a haven for hikers and nature lovers, offering a network of trails that traverse the park's varied terrain, revealing spectacular views of the rugged coastline and the serene beauty of remote villages.

The park is distinguished by its remarkable biodiversity. Home to many endemic species of flora and fauna, Anaga Rural Park is a living laboratory for the study of Tenerife's unique ecological heritage. The trails range in difficulty, catering to both seasoned hikers and those seeking a leisurely walk amidst nature.

Tip: Begin your exploration at the visitor center at Cruz del Carmen, where you can gather information on trails and sign up for guided tours. Essential for the journey are comfortable hiking shoes and adequate water to stay hydrated.

Location: Northeastern Tenerife - Afur, Santa Cruz de Tenerife, Spain (coord: 28°32'43.3"N 16°13'43.4"W)
Website: www.reservabiosfera.tenerife.es

SANTA CRUZ DE TENERIFE

Santa Cruz de Tenerife, the dynamic capital of the island, is a delightful blend of old-world charm and modern vibrancy. This bustling city is a treasure trove of experiences, boasting an array of historical architecture, cutting-edge arts, and lively markets. One of its architectural gems is the Auditorio de Tenerife, a contemporary structure that has become an emblem of the city's skyline. Equally fascinating is the Museo de la Naturaleza y el Hombre, where visitors can delve into the natural history and archaeology of the Canary Islands.

Santa Cruz is also celebrated for its spirited festivals, most notably the Carnival of Santa Cruz de Tenerife, one of the world's largest and most vibrant. The city's streets come alive with music, dance, and elaborate costumes, drawing visitors from around the globe.

Tip: To truly experience the city's essence, wander through its diverse neighborhoods, each offering a distinct character and charm. A visit to the Mercado Nuestra Señora de África is a must for food enthusiasts. This bustling market is the heart of the city's culinary scene, offering a taste of local flavors and delicacies.

Location: Northeastern coast of Tenerife - Santa Cruz de Tenerife, Tenerife, Spain
Website: www.spain.info/en/destination/santa-cruz-tenerife/

LA GOMERA

Embarking on a day trip to La Gomera from Tenerife unveils a world of natural splendor and cultural richness. This neighboring island, a UNESCO Biosphere Reserve, captivates visitors with its pristine beauty and unique traditions. La Gomera is renowned for its ancient laurel forests, which envelop much of the island in lush greenery, and its dramatic cliffs that offer stunning views of the Atlantic Ocean.

A visit to Garajonay National Park, the heart of the island's natural heritage, is a must. This park is home to a diversity of flora and fauna, and its misty forests create a mystical atmosphere. The charming village of San Sebastián de La Gomera, steeped in history, offers a glimpse into the island's past and culture. Additionally, La Gomera is known for its unique whistling language, Silbo Gomero, used by the locals for centuries.

Tip: To gain a deeper understanding of La Gomera's rich history, culture, and natural landscapes, consider taking a guided tour. The ferry journey from Los Cristianos in Tenerife to La Gomera itself is an experience, presenting breathtaking vistas of the ocean and neighboring islands.

Location: Accessible by ferry from Los Cristianos in Tenerife
Website: www.lagomera.travel

HIDDEN GEMS AND LESSER-KNOWN SIGHTS IN TENERIFE
PUNTA DE TENO

Punta de Teno, located at the westernmost tip of Tenerife, is a breathtakingly beautiful and lesser-known spot on the island. This remote headland offers some of the most spectacular views Tenerife has to offer, with the majestic Los Gigantes cliffs and the serene island of La Gomera in the distance. The area's rugged and untouched landscape is crowned by a picturesque lighthouse, adding to its scenic charm.

For visitors seeking a peaceful retreat from the island's busier tourist areas, Punta de Teno is an ideal destination. It provides a perfect setting for various outdoor activities like hiking, bird watching, and simply enjoying nature's wonders. The sunsets here are particularly memorable, painting the sky and sea in vibrant hues.

Tip: Access to Punta de Teno can be limited, as the road is often closed to private vehicles, especially on weekends and holidays, to protect this delicate environment. To visit, consider using the public bus service or plan your trip on a weekday to ensure easier access.

Location: 38480 Buenavista del Nte., Santa Cruz de Tenerife, Spain
Website: www.hellocanaryislands.com/nature-spaces/tenerife/teno-rural-park/

BARRANCO DEL INFIERNO

Barranco del Infierno, aptly named "Hell's Gorge," is a hidden natural treasure nestled in the town of Adeje, Tenerife. This stunning ravine is renowned for its extraordinary natural beauty and rich biodiversity, offering one of the most enchanting hiking experiences on the island. The trail, approximately 6.5 km in total, winds through the gorge on ancient paths that reveal the diverse flora and fauna of Tenerife.

A standout feature of this hike is the striking waterfall at the trail's end, a rare and captivating sight in Tenerife's arid landscape. This journey through Barranco del Infierno not only provides a physical adventure but also a journey through the natural history of the island, with every turn offering a new and breathtaking view.

Tip: Due to environmental protection efforts, access to the trail is limited to a specific number of visitors each day. It is highly recommended to book your ticket in advance to secure your spot and avoid disappointment.

Location: Adeje, Santa Cruz de Tenerife, Spain (coord: 28°07'32.9"N 16°43'18.2"W)
Website: www.barrancodelinfierno.es/en/

CUEVA DEL VIENTO

Cueva del Viento, known as the "Cave of the Wind", is a remarkable geological wonder located in Icod de los Vinos, Tenerife. It stands as one of the largest volcanic tubes in the world, a mesmerizing creation of nature formed by ancient lava flows from Pico Viejo, near Mount Teide. This subterranean marvel offers a unique adventure into the depths of the Earth.

Guided tours provide an exclusive opportunity to explore a portion of this extensive underground labyrinth. The journey through Cueva del Viento is an educational and exhilarating experience, showcasing an array of unique geological formations, intriguing fossils, and a diverse range of fauna adapted to the darkness of the cave environment.

Visitors will be captivated by the mysterious and otherworldly atmosphere within the cave, offering a stark contrast to the sunny landscapes above ground. The tour is both informative and thrilling, revealing the hidden wonders beneath Tenerife's surface.

Tip: For a comfortable experience, wear sturdy shoes and bring a jacket, as the cave's temperature is cooler. Photography is permitted, but flash is prohibited to protect the delicate ecosystem of the cave.

Location: Cam. los Piquetes, 51, 38438 Icod de los Vinos, Santa Cruz de Tenerife, Spain
Website: www.cuevadelviento.net/en/home/

LA OROTAVA

La Orotava, a charming town in North Tenerife, is a hidden gem steeped in history and natural beauty. Nestled in a lush, fertile valley, this town is renowned for its exquisitely preserved historical center, where traditional Canarian architecture is showcased in all its glory. As you wander through its cobblestone streets, the town's character unfolds in the form of stunning gardens and intricately carved wooden balconies, characteristic of the local style.

A visit to La Orotava offers more than just a walk through history. The town serves as a gateway to the majestic Teide National Park, making it an ideal stop for nature lovers and explorers. Key attractions include the historic Casa de los Balcones, a prime example of Canarian architecture, providing an insight into the island's cultural heritage.

Tip: Be sure to visit Victoria Gardens and Hijuela del Botánico. These gardens are among the town's most picturesque spots, offering serene landscapes and a variety of plant species, perfect for a relaxing stroll or a picnic.

Location: North Tenerife La Orotava, Tenerife, Spain
Website: www.laorotava.es

PLAYA DEL DUQUE

Playa del Duque, nestled in the upscale area of Costa Adeje, Tenerife, is a pristine and somewhat hidden beach that offers a luxurious and peaceful seaside experience. Distinct for its golden sands and clear blue waters, this beach is a haven for those seeking a serene day by the ocean. Its well-maintained environment and the quality of the amenities contribute to a sense of exclusivity and tranquility.

Adding to the allure of Playa del Duque is the elegant promenade that runs alongside it. This promenade is lined with chic cafes and high-end boutiques, providing visitors with a variety of options for dining and shopping. The beach's atmosphere is relaxed and sophisticated, making it an ideal spot for those looking to escape the more crowded and bustling beaches on the island.

Tip: To enhance your beach experience, consider renting a sunbed and umbrella. This not only ensures comfort throughout the day but also provides a prime spot to enjoy the breathtaking sunset views that this beach is known for.

Location: 38679 Playa del Duque, Santa Cruz de Tenerife, Spain (coord: 28°05'29.2"N 16°44'38.1"W)
Website:
www.hellocanaryislands.com/beaches/tenerife/playa-del-duque/

ARTLANDYA

ARTlandya, nestled in the serene rural area of Icod de los Vinos in Tenerife, is a delightful and unique museum that stands as a testament to the timeless art of doll making and teddy bear craftsmanship. This museum is a hidden gem, offering a charming and somewhat unexpected experience for visitors to the island.

The museum houses an extensive and meticulously curated collection of handmade dolls and teddy bears from various parts of the world. Each piece in the collection showcases the intricate skills and creative artistry involved in this traditional craft. ARTlandya is not just a museum; it's a journey into the whimsical world of childhood nostalgia and the fine art of doll and teddy bear creation.

Tip: Enhance your visit with a guided tour, where you can learn about the fascinating process behind doll making. After the tour, take time to wander in the museum's beautifully landscaped garden, which adds to the tranquil and enchanting atmosphere of the place.

Location: Cam. el Moleiro, 21, 38430 Icod de los Vinos, Santa Cruz de Tenerife, Spain
Website: www.artlandya.com

CHARCO DE LA LAJA

Nestled in the quaint town of San Juan de la Rambla in northern Tenerife, Charco de La Laja stands as a hidden gem in the island's diverse landscape. This natural seawater pool, shaped by the forces of volcanic lava flows, offers a unique and exhilarating swimming experience that contrasts sharply with the conventional beach setting. The crystal-clear waters of the pool provide a serene spot for a refreshing swim, surrounded by the dramatic and rugged beauty of Tenerife's volcanic coastline.

The raw power of the Atlantic Ocean is evident here, as waves crash against the rocks, creating a spectacular natural display. The pool's location makes it a relatively secluded spot, ideal for those seeking tranquility away from the more crowded tourist areas.

Tip: For a safe and enjoyable experience, it's recommended to visit Charco de La Laja during low tide when the swimming conditions are more favorable. Wearing water shoes is advisable due to the rocky nature of the pool. Additionally, the site becomes particularly magical during sunset, offering stunning views and photo opportunities.

Location: C. Antonio Ruiz Cedrés, 47, 38420 San Juan de la Rambla, Santa Cruz de Tenerife, Spain
Website: www.hellocanaryislands.com/natural-pools/tenerife/charco-de-la-laja/

VILAFLOR DE CHASNA TENERIFE

Perched at the highest altitude of any village in Tenerife, Vilaflor de Chasna is a captivating destination that offers more than just its lofty elevation. This picturesque village is enveloped in a blanket of tranquil pine forests and lush vineyards, creating a serene and verdant landscape that beckons nature lovers and peace seekers alike. Its unique position makes it an ideal starting point for exploring the surrounding natural wonders, including the surreal and otherworldly Paisaje Lunar, known for its moon-like terrain.

The charm of Vilaflor de Chasna extends to its village streets, where traditional Canarian architecture is displayed in all its glory. The buildings, with their quaint and rustic appeal, add to the historical and cultural ambiance of the village. Walking through Vilaflor, visitors are treated to an authentic Canarian experience, far removed from the bustling tourist centers.

Tip: A visit to Vilaflor is incomplete without tasting the local wines. The high-altitude vineyards of the area impart a distinct character and flavor to the wines, making them a must-try for oenophiles and casual wine enthusiasts alike.

Location: Vilaflor, Santa Cruz de Tenerife, Spain
Website: www.webtenerife.com/tenerife/la-isla/municipios/vilaflor

MONTAÑA ROJA NATURAL RESERVE

Montaña Roja Natural Reserve, a remarkable natural attraction near El Médano in Tenerife, is famed for its distinctive volcanic cone, known as Montaña Roja or "Red Mountain". This protected area is a sanctuary for wildlife enthusiasts and nature lovers, boasting a rich array of bird species and indigenous flora. The hike to the summit of Montaña Roja is a relatively easy endeavor, making it accessible for most fitness levels, and it rewards hikers with spectacular panoramic views of the stunning coastline and the azure waters of the Atlantic Ocean.

Adjacent to this natural reserve is a lesser-known attraction, the Montaña Roja Beach, which is popular among nudists. This secluded beach offers a tranquil and natural environment, characterized by its fine sand and clear waters, making it an ideal spot for those seeking a more private beach experience.

Tip: Don't forget to bring binoculars for a rewarding birdwatching experience and a camera to capture the stunning vistas from the summit. The natural reserve and the adjacent beach both offer unique experiences worth exploring.

Location: 38618, Santa Cruz de Tenerife, Spain
Website: www.spain.info/en/beach/montana-roja-granadilla-abona/

PARKS AND GARDENS IN TENERIFE

LAGO MARTIÁNEZ

Lago Martiánez, situated in the vibrant city of Puerto de la Cruz, is not just a swimming complex but a true work of art, conceptualized by the renowned Canarian artist César Manrique. This striking open-air water park beautifully merges art, architecture, and the natural landscape, creating an oasis of tranquility and aesthetic pleasure. At the heart of the complex lies a large artificial lake, surrounded by various sea-water pools, each offering a refreshing dip with picturesque views of the Atlantic Ocean.

The park's design is complemented by lush gardens, inviting terraces, and intriguing sculptures, all contributing to an atmosphere that is both relaxing and culturally enriching. Lago Martiánez is more than just a place to swim; it's a destination that provides a unique experience, combining leisure with an appreciation for artistic design.

Tip: For an enchanting experience, visit Lago Martiánez in the evening. The pools are beautifully illuminated, creating a magical ambiance. Enjoying a cocktail at one of the terraced bars while overlooking the illuminated waters is a perfect way to end a day in Puerto de la Cruz.

Location: Av. de Cristobal Colón, s/n, 38400 Puerto de la Cruz, Santa Cruz de Tenerife, Spain

Website: www.lagomartianez.es/en/

PALMETUM OF SANTA CRUZ

The Palmetum is a botanical garden in Santa Cruz de Tenerife dedicated to palm trees. This 12-hectare park, built on a former landfill, is now a beautiful space showcasing one of the most important collections of palm trees in the world. The garden is divided into biogeographical sections, representing different parts of the world. Besides palms, it includes lakes, streams, and a variety of other tropical and subtropical plant species.

Tip: Climb to the highest point of the garden for a panoramic view of the city and the sea.
Location: Av. la Constitución, 5, 38005 Santa Cruz de Tenerife, Spain
Website: www.palmetumtenerife.es/?lang=en

RURAL PARK OF TENO

The Rural Park of Teno, located in the northwestern part of Tenerife, is an area of exceptional natural beauty, characterized by its rugged mountains, deep ravines, and rich biodiversity. The park is a popular spot for hiking and bird watching, with trails leading to remote villages like Masca and Teno Alto. The landscape offers a glimpse into the geological history of the island and is a perfect place for those seeking an off-the-beaten-path experience.

Tip: The roads to the park are narrow and winding, so drive cautiously. Consider visiting the Punta de Teno lighthouse for stunning coastal views.
Location: Buenavista del Norte, Santa Cruz de Tenerife,
Website: www.webtenerife.co.uk/what-see/outdoor-attractions/teno-country-park

BOTANICAL GARDENS (JARDIN BOTANICO)

The Botanical Gardens, or Jardín de Aclimatación de La Orotava, located in Puerto de la Cruz, Tenerife, are a treasure trove of botanical wonders. Established in the late 18th century, these gardens serve as a historical and botanical landmark. They were originally intended for acclimatizing tropical plants to the European environment, and today, they continue to flourish as a testament to this historical purpose.

As visitors stroll through the gardens, they are enveloped in an atmosphere of peace and natural beauty. The collection includes an impressive array of tropical and subtropical plant species. Majestic trees, some centuries old, exotic flowers bursting with vibrant colors, and an assortment of palm species create a lush, green sanctuary that feels worlds away from the bustling city life.

Tip: Be sure to seek out the garden's oldest resident, a majestic 200-year-old fig tree, and marvel at the giant bird of paradise plants, which are among the most striking attractions of the gardens.

Location: C. Retama, 2, 38400 Puerto de la Cruz, Santa Cruz de Tenerife, Spain.
Website: www.webtenerife.co.uk/what-see/gardens-and-parks/jardin-botanico/

SITIO LITRE ORCHID GARDEN

Sitio Litre, located in Puerto de la Cruz, is home to the oldest garden in Tenerife and hosts the island's largest collection of orchids. This lush, tranquil garden offers a serene escape, with its vibrant array of orchids, towering dragon trees, and a variety of tropical plants. The garden's history dates back to the 18th century and includes a charming manor house that adds to the site's historical charm.

Tip: Look for the famous 'Orchid Wall', a stunning display of various orchid species in full bloom.
Location: Cam. Sitio Litre, 16, 38400 Puerto de la Cruz, Santa Cruz de Tenerife, Spain
Website: www.jardindeorquideas.com/en

GARCÍA SANABRIA PARK TENERIFE

García Sanabria Park, the largest urban green space in the Canary Islands, is a picturesque oasis in the heart of Santa Cruz de Tenerife. Named after a former mayor, this urban park blends nature, art, and leisure with its manicured gardens, meandering paths, and diverse outdoor sculptures. It features a unique floral clock, a symbol of the park, and lush tropical foliage. The park is a beloved destination for both locals and tourists, ideal for strolls, picnics, and enjoying the peaceful atmosphere.

Tip: Check out the park's cultural events and exhibitions, particularly in the warmer months.

Location: Rbla. de Sta. Cruz, Santa Cruz de Tenerife, Spain
Website: www.webtenerife.co.uk/what-see/gardens-and-parks/parque-garcia-sanabria/

TENERIFE'S CULINARY SCENE

GUACHINCHES

Guachinches are traditional eateries unique to Tenerife, offering an authentic dining experience. They are typically small, family-run establishments serving homemade Canarian dishes and local wines. Guachinches are known for their rustic charm and warm hospitality, providing an intimate glimpse into the island's culinary culture. Dishes to try include "ropa vieja" (a hearty stew), grilled meats, and "papas arrugadas" (wrinkly potatoes) with mojo sauce.

Tip: Guachinches often have limited opening times and seasons, so check in advance. They're great places for an affordable, authentic meal.

Location: Various locations, primarily in the northern Tenerife
Website: www.guachinchestenerife.com

EL CALDERITO DE LA ABUELA

El Calderito de la Abuela is a renowned restaurant in Santa Úrsula, offering a blend of traditional Canarian cuisine and modern culinary techniques. The restaurant boasts spectacular views of Mount Teide and the ocean, providing a perfect backdrop for a memorable dining experience. Their menu includes local specialties made with fresh, locally sourced ingredients.

Tip: Try their signature dishes like "cabrito en salsa" (goat in sauce) and the variety of homemade desserts.

Location: Carr. Provincial, 130, 38390 Cuesta de la Villa, Santa Cruz de Tenerife, Spain
Website: www.elcalderitodelaabuela.net

TASCA TIERRAS DEL SUR

Tasca Tierras del Sur is a charming restaurant located in Granadilla de Abona. It's celebrated for its creative approach to Canarian cuisine, combining traditional recipes with contemporary flair. The restaurant's cozy and inviting atmosphere, coupled with its innovative dishes, makes it a favorite among locals and visitors alike.

Tip: Be sure to try their "pulpo a la gallega" (Galician-style octopus) and the selection of local cheeses.
Location: C. Pedro González Gómez, 20, 38600 Granadilla, Santa Cruz de Tenerife, Spain
Website: www.tascatierrasdelsur.com/en/

RESTAURANTE OTELO

Restaurante Otelo is famous for its "pollo al ajillo" (garlic chicken), a dish that has drawn locals and tourists alike for years. Located near the Barranco del Infierno in Adeje, this restaurant offers a simple yet delicious menu in a rustic setting. The terrace provides a beautiful view of the surrounding valley.

Tip: After enjoying your meal, take a stroll in the nearby Barranco del lInfierno to experience one of Tenerife's stunning natural landscapes.

Location: C. de los Molinos, 44, 38670 Adeje, Santa Cruz de Tenerife, Spain

Website: www.otelorestaurante.com/en/

CONEJO EN SALMOREJO

Conejo en Salmorejo, rabbit in salmorejo sauce, is a quintessential dish in Tenerife's cuisine. This flavorful and hearty meal combines tender rabbit meat with salmorejo, a rich marinade made from garlic, paprika, vinegar, and spices. The dish is a testament to the island's love for game meats and robust, aromatic flavors. **Serving Style**: The rabbit is marinated in the salmorejo sauce before being fried or grilled, resulting in meat that's infused with deep flavors and a slightly tangy finish. **Where to Try**: This traditional dish is best enjoyed in rustic "guachinches" or local eateries, where it's often served as part of a larger meal featuring other Canarian specialties. **Tip**: Pair conejo en salmorejo with a local red wine or a cold beer to complement the rich flavors of the dish.

GOFIO

Gofio, a staple in the Canarian diet, is a versatile and nutritious flour made from toasted grains, typically wheat or maize. This traditional food, deeply rooted in Tenerife's culinary heritage, has been nourishing the island's inhabitants for centuries. Gofio is celebrated for its earthy flavor and is used in various dishes,  from soups and stews to desserts, showcasing its adaptability in both savory and sweet preparations. **Serving Style**: Gofio can be found mixed into stews for thickening, kneaded into dough for bread, or even blended with honey and almonds to create a sweet dessert. **Where to Try**: Experience gofio in traditional Canarian restaurants across Tenerife, where it's often used as a key ingredient in many local dishes. **Tip**: For a truly authentic taste, try gofio amasado - a simple yet satisfying dish where gofio is mixed with water, salt, and sometimes honey or cheese, forming a dense dough

BARRAQUITO

Barraquito is a beloved coffee concoction unique to the Canary Islands, particularly Tenerife. This layered coffee drink is not only a delight for the taste buds but also a visual treat. It combines coffee, milk, Licor 43 (a citrus-flavored Spanish liqueur), lemon, cinnamon, and sometimes a touch of condensed milk, creating a rich and aromatic beverage that reflects the island's love for intricate coffee preparations.

Serving Style: The ingredients are carefully layered in a small glass, creating distinct layers that blend together when stirred. It's usually served warm and often enjoyed as a mid-morning or after-lunch drink. **Where to Try**: Barraquito can be found in most cafes across Tenerife, each adding their own twist to this classic drink. **Tip**: For the full experience, sip it slowly to enjoy the different flavors as they combine, and don't forget to stir it before drinking to blend the layers harmoniously.

BIENMESABE

Bienmesabe, which translates to "tastes good to me," is a traditional Canarian dessert known for its sweet, rich flavor. This almond-based treat is typically made with ground almonds, egg yolks, sugar, lemon zest, and cinnamon. It's a staple in Tenerife's culinary scene and showcases the island's penchant for using locally sourced ingredients in their desserts.

Serving Style: Bienmesabe is often served cold and accompanied by a scoop of ice cream or a dollop of fresh cream, enhancing its creamy texture and rich flavors. **Where to Try**: This dessert is a common feature in many restaurants and dessert shops throughout Tenerife, especially in areas known for their traditional Canarian cuisine. **Tip**: Enjoy bienmesabe as a perfect ending to a meal of local dishes, allowing the sweet and nutty flavors to complement the savory notes of the Canarian gastronomy.

PAPAS ARRUGADAS WITH MOJO SAUCE

Papas Arrugadas with Mojo Sauce is a signature dish of the Canary Islands, embodying the simplicity and flavor of Tenerife's cuisine. These "wrinkled potatoes" are small, salty, and cooked in their skins, creating a unique texture. The dish is elevated with the addition of Mojo Sauce, a garlicky and sometimes spicy condiment, traditionally served in two varieties: Mojo Rojo (red) and Mojo Verde (green). **Serving Style**: The potatoes are boiled in saltwater until tender and then baked until their skins wrinkle. They are typically served with both types of Mojo Sauce, offering a harmonious blend of flavors. **Where to Try**: Papas Arrugadas with Mojo Sauce is a staple in most local restaurants across Tenerife, particularly in traditional eateries known as "guachinches." **Tip**: For a truly authentic experience, enjoy this dish as part of a tapas meal, allowing you to savor the variety of flavors alongside other local specialties.

QUESO ASADO

Queso Asado, translating to "grilled cheese," is a beloved delicacy in Tenerife's culinary repertoire. This dish features a thick slice of local goat cheese, typically from the Canary Islands, grilled or roasted to perfection. The outer layer becomes crispy and golden, while the inside remains soft and creamy. **Serving Style**: The cheese is often served with a drizzle of palm honey or a spicy Mojo Sauce, creating a delightful contrast of flavors. **Where to Try**: Queso Asado can be found in many restaurants across Tenerife, especially those that focus on traditional Canarian cuisine. **Tip**: Pair this dish with a local wine, such as a crisp white from the region, to enhance the flavors and complete your culinary experience.

SHOPPING IN TENERIFE

LOCAL MARKETS

Tenerife's local markets are vibrant hubs of activity where you can experience the island's culture and shop for fresh produce, artisan crafts, and unique souvenirs. These markets, found in various towns across the island, offer everything from fresh fruits and vegetables to handmade jewelry, clothing, and traditional Canarian products. **Where to Find**: Notable markets include Mercado del Agricultor in Tacoronte, Mercadillo del Agricultor in Los Cristianos, and Mercado Municipal in La Laguna.

Tip: Visit early in the morning for the best selection of fresh produce and try some local cheeses and wines available at many market stalls.

Website: www.hellocanaryislands.com/shopping/tenerife/

MERCADO DE NUESTRA SEÑORA DE ÁFRICA

The Mercado de Nuestra Señora de África, also known as "La Recova", is a bustling market in the heart of Santa Cruz de Tenerife. This market is a feast for the senses, offering an array of fresh produce, meats, fish, spices, and flowers. It's housed in a beautiful building, with a clock tower that's an iconic feature of the city. In addition to food, the market has stalls selling clothes, accessories, and handicrafts. **Tip**: Be sure to visit the market's food court for a taste of local cuisine, including fresh seafood dishes and typical Canarian snacks.

Location: Av. de San Sebastián, 51, 38003 Santa Cruz de Tenerife, Spain

Website: www.la-recova.com

EL CORTE INGLÉS

El Corte Inglés is Spain's largest department store chain and offers a comprehensive shopping experience. In Tenerife, this store provides a variety of products, ranging from clothing and accessories to electronics, homeware, and gourmet food. Known for its quality and variety, it's a one-stop shop for both locals and tourists. The store also features a supermarket and several dining options.

Tip: Check out their gourmet section for local Spanish and Canarian delicacies, which make great gifts or souvenirs.
Location: Av. Tres de Mayo, 7, 38003 Santa Cruz de Tenerife, Spain
Website: www.elcorteingles.es

SIAM MALL

Siam Mall, located near the popular Siam Park, is a modern shopping center offering a wide range of shops, from well-known international brands to local boutiques. This open-air mall, with its contemporary design and pleasant ambiance, is ideal for a day of shopping. It also has a variety of restaurants and cafes, as well as regular events and activities for all ages.

Tip: Visit the terrace for dining options with a view, and keep an eye on their calendar for family-friendly events and live entertainment.
Location: Av. Siam, 3, 38670 Costa Adeje, Santa Cruz de Tenerife, Spain
Website: www.ccsiammall.com/?lang=en

LA LAGUNA'S HISTORIC CENTRE

The historic center of San Cristobal de La Laguna, a UNESCO World Heritage Site, is not only a place of rich history and culture but also a delightful shopping area. The streets are lined with small shops, boutiques, and artisan workshops where you can find unique clothing, handicrafts, books, and more. The area is pedestrian-friendly, making it a pleasant place to stroll and explore.

Tip: Visit the local artisan shops for handcrafted items that reflect the cultural heritage of the Canary Islands.
Location: San Cristobal de La Laguna, North Tenerife
Website: www.hellocanaryislands.com/places-full-of-charm/tenerife/la-laguna-old-town/

PLAZA DEL DUQUE SHOPPING CENTER

Plaza del Duque, located in the upscale area of Costa Adeje, is Tenerife's premier shopping destination for luxury and high-end brands. This stylish and modern shopping center boasts an elegant atmosphere and a selection of international designer stores, boutiques, and local artisan shops. It offers a diverse shopping experience, catering to those with a taste for fashion, jewelry, and fine goods. The center's architectural design, complete with soothing water features and a relaxed ambiance, makes for an enjoyable shopping experience.

Tip: After shopping, enjoy a meal or a coffee at one of the plaza's upscale cafes and restaurants, where you can relax and soak in the luxurious surroundings.
Location: C. Londres, s/n, 38660 Costa Adeje, Santa Cruz de Tenerife, Spain
Website: www.plazadelduque.com/?lang=en

FAMILY-FRIENDLY ACTIVITIES IN TENERIFE

AQUALAND COSTA ADEJE

Aqualand Costa Adeje is a water park that combines thrilling water slides and attractions with a dedicated kid's area, making it an ideal destination for families. The park features a range of slides, from adrenaline-pumping to more relaxed options, as well as a wave pool and lazy river. One of the highlights is the Dolphin Show, renowned for its impressive display of acrobatics and intelligence by the resident dolphins.

Tip: Plan to visit the dolphin show early in the day as it's a popular attraction and seats fill up quickly.
Location: Av. Austria, 15, 38660 Costa Adeje, Santa Cruz de Tenerife, Spain
Website: www.aqualand.es/costa-adeje/en/

JUNGLE PARK

Jungle Park, also known as Las Águilas Jungle Park, is a zoological and botanical park located in Arona. This park is home to a wide variety of animals, including exotic birds, primates, big cats, and more. The park offers several shows, including an exotic bird show and a birds of prey show, which are both educational and entertaining. The lush surroundings make it feel like a jungle adventure, perfect for family exploration.

Tip: Don't miss the bird of prey show, which features eagles and falcons in free flight, showcasing their incredible hunting skills.
Location: Urb. Águilas del Teide, s/n, Km. 3, 38640 Arona, Santa Cruz de Tenerife, Spain
Website: www.junglepark.es

MONKEY PARK

Monkey Park is an interactive zoo focusing on primate conservation. It offers a unique experience where visitors can interact closely with some of the animals, including feeding and petting them. The park hosts a variety of species, including monkeys, lemurs, iguanas, and birds. It's an educational and fun experience for  allowing them to learn about different species and the importance of wildlife conservation.

Tip: Buy a bag of food at the entrance to feed the animals, making for  a more interactive experience. Remember to follow the staff's guidelines for safe and respectful interactions.
Location: Camino Moreque,Llano Azul,17, Tf662 Km 2, 38627, Santa Cruz de Tenerife, Spain
Website: www.monkeypark.com

SUBMARINE DIVES

Submarine dives offer a unique underwater adventure for the whole family. Operated by Submarine Safaris, these dives take place in a real submarine, providing a rare opportunity to explore Tenerife's underwater world without getting wet. The submarine dives to depths of about 30 meters, where you can see  various marine life, shipwrecks, and the fascinating volcanic seabed. This activity is both thrilling and educational, making it perfect for curious minds.

 **Tip**: The submarine is equipped with large viewing ports, ensuring great visibility for all passengers. Bring a camera for some unique underwater photos.
Location: Marina San Miguel, 38639, Santa Cruz de Tenerife, Spain
Website: www.submarinesafaris.com

SNORKELING AND KAYAKING ADVENTURES

Tenerife's clear waters and abundant marine life make it an excellent destination for snorkeling and kayaking. Various companies offer guided tours, suitable for families, to explore the coast and encounter marine life such as turtles and dolphins in their natural habitat. These activities are not only fun but also provide an opportunity to learn about marine conservation and the importance of protecting ocean life.
Tip: Look for tours that provide all necessary equipment and cater to all experience levels ensuring a safe and enjoyable adventure for the whole family.
Location: Calle el Coronel no. 1, Edificio Cristianmar local 10, 38650 Los Cristianos, Tenerife
Website: www.xploretenerife.com

SUNSET AND STARGAZING IN TEIDE

Experience the majestic beauty of Mount Teide at sunset followed by an awe-inspiring stargazing session. These tours take you up the mountain in the late afternoon, allowing you to witness the stunning colors of sunset over the volcanic landscape. As night falls, the clear skies of Teide National Park offer perfect conditions for stargazing. Guided by astronomy experts, you can observe constellations, planets, and stars through telescopes.
Tip: Dress warmly as temperatures drop significantly after sunset at high altitudes. Bringing a camera with a night mode can capture some spectacular shots of the night sky.
Location: Teide National Park, Central Tenerife
Website: www.volcanoteide.com/en

TENERIFE BY NIGHT

ILLUMINATED MONUMENTS AND EVENING STROLLS

PLAZA DE ESPAÑA IN SANTA CRUZ

Plaza de España is the largest square in Santa Cruz de Tenerife and a hub of evening activity. Illuminated at night, the plaza and its surroundings, including the Monument to the Fallen, become a spectacle of light and shadow. The area is perfect for an evening stroll, with several cafes and restaurants nearby. The adjacent marina also offers beautiful nighttime views.

Tip: Enjoy a leisurely walk along the marina and visit the nearby Calle Castillo for some late-night shopping or dining.
Location: Santa Cruz de Tenerife, North Tenerife
Website: www.spain.info/en/destination/santa-cruz-tenerife/

LA LAGUNA AT NIGHT

The historic city of La Laguna, with its UNESCO-listed old town, transforms into a lively spot at night. The streets are beautifully lit, highlighting the colonial architecture and creating a magical atmosphere. It's a great place to explore on foot, with many bars, restaurants, and cafes that cater to the city's vibrant student population.

Tip: Visit the local tapas bars for an authentic Canarian culinary experience and enjoy the lively atmosphere of this historic town.
Location: San Cristobal de La Laguna, North Tenerife
Website: www.spain.info/en/destination/san-cristobal-laguna/

PLAYA DE LAS AMERICAS

Playa de las Americas is known for its vibrant nightlife, and a walk along its promenade at night is a delightful experience. The area is lined with bars, clubs, and restaurants, all illuminated and bustling with activity. The beach itself, lit by the lights of the promenade and nearby resorts, offers a serene backdrop to the lively atmosphere.

Tip: The promenade is family-friendly and offers a variety of entertainment options, from live music to street performers.
Location: Playa de las Americas, South Tenerife
Website: www.hellocanaryislands.com/tourist-resorts/tenerife/playa-de-las-americas/

TEIDE BY NIGHT

A night tour of Teide National Park offers an unforgettable experience under the stars. Teide is one of the best places in the world for stargazing due to its high altitude and clear skies. Guided tours often include a sunset view from the mountain followed by stargazing with telescopes and expert astronomers who explain the constellations and celestial phenomena.

Tip: Dress warmly as temperatures can be quite low at night, and bring a camera capable of night photography to capture the stunning night sky.
Location: Teide National Park, Central Tenerife
Website: www.teidebynight.com

BARS AND PUBS

PAPAGAYO BEACH CLUB

Papagayo Beach Club is one of the most stylish and popular spots in Tenerife for a night out. Located right on the beachfront in Playa de las Américas, it offers a sophisticated ambiance with stunning ocean views. The club features a restaurant, cocktail bar, and a dance floor, with DJs playing a mix of house, electronic, and popular music.

It's a perfect place for those looking to enjoy a chic evening of dining, dancing, and cocktails. **Tip**: Visit during sunset for an unforgettable experience as you watch the sky change colors over the ocean with a cocktail in hand.

Location: Av. Rafael Puig Lluvina, 2, 38650 Playa de la Américas, Santa Cruz de Tenerife, Spain
Website: www.papagayobeachclub.com/en

MONKEY BEACH CLUB

Monkey Beach Club, located near the golden sands of Playa de Troya, is a vibrant venue known for its lively atmosphere and beachside party scene. It offers a mix of dining, music, and entertainment, with a diverse program of events, including live DJ sets, themed parties, and special performances. The club's terrace is ideal for enjoying a drink while overlooking the sea.

Tip: Check their events calendar for special themed nights or guest DJ performances, which are a major draw for both locals and tourists.

Location: Av. Rafael Puig Lluvina, 3, 38660 Arona, Santa Cruz de Tenerife, Spain
Website: www.monkeybeachclub.com

DEL DIEGO COCKTAIL BAR

Lounge, situated in the heart of Playa de las Américas, is a sophisticated and trendy spot that offers a classy nightlife experience. Known for its elegant decor and relaxed atmosphere, this lounge bar specializes in creative cocktails and premium spirits. It's a popular destination for those seeking a more refined evening out, with a backdrop of smooth lounge music and occasional live performances.

Location: 1st floor Commercial Centre Safari, Av. las Américas, 38650 Playa de la Américas, Santa Cruz de Tenerife, Spain
Website: www.biancorestauranttenerife.com

EL BÚHO LA LAGUNA

El Búho, nestled in the historic town of La Laguna, offers a cozy and intimate atmosphere for a night out. This charming bar is known for its rustic interior, live music sessions, and a wide selection of local and international beers and wines. It's an ideal spot for those looking to unwind in a more laid-back environment, away from the bustling club scene. The bar also features an array of tapas and light bites, perfect for sharing.

Tip: Check out their live music nights for an entertaining experience featuring local bands and artists. The outdoor seating is great for enjoying the lively streets of La Laguna.
Location: Calle Catedral, 3, 38205 La Laguna, Santa Cruz de Tenerife, Spain
Website: www.instagram.com/elbuholalaguna/

NIGHTCLUBS AND DANCE CLUBS

TRAMPS THE KING OF CLUBS

Tramps The King of Clubs is one of the most renowned nightclubs in Tenerife, known for its vibrant atmosphere and top-quality entertainment. Located in Playa de las Américas, it features multiple dance floors, each offering different music genres, from house and techno to R&B and hip hop. The club regularly hosts international DJs and themed party nights, making it a go-to spot for a lively night out.

Tip: Keep an eye on their event schedule for guest DJ nights and special events, which are particularly popular and often attract a large crowd.

Location: Centro Comercial Starco, Avenida Arquitecto Gómez Cuesta, s/n, 38660 Playa de las Américas, Santa Cruz de Tenerife, Spain

Website: www.trampstenerife.com

MAGIC LOUNGE CLUB

Magic Lounge Club, also in Playa de las Américas, offers a sophisticated nightlife experience with its elegant decor, extensive cocktail menu, and live DJ sets. It's a place where you can enjoy a more relaxed evening with lounge music early in the night, which gradually transitions into a vibrant dance scene as the night progresses.

Tip: Try their signature cocktails, created by expert mixologists, and enjoy the terrace area for a more intimate setting.

Location: Mare Nostrum Resort, Av. las Américas, s/n, 38660 Playa de la Américas, Santa Cruz de Tenerife, Spain

Website: www.magicbartenerife.com

ACHAMAN DISCOPUB

Achaman Discopub is a lively spot in the heart of the Playa de las Américas nightlife district. Known for its friendly atmosphere and energetic music, the club features a mix of Latin, Spanish, and international hits. It's a great place to dance the night away, especially if you enjoy Latin rhythms like salsa and reggaeton.

Tip: The club often hosts Latin dance nights and live performances, so check their schedule for a night of energetic dancing.
Location: Av. Francisco Ucelay Sabina, 38660 Costa Adeje, Santa Cruz de Tenerife, Spain
Website: www.facebook.com/achamandiscopub/

ENVY

Envy is a trendy nightclub that stands out for its stylish interior and lively party scene. Located in Costa Adeje, it attracts a younger crowd with its modern sound system and lighting, playing a mix of the latest hits and electronic dance music. The club also features themed nights and guest DJ performances.

Tip: Visit on a themed night for a unique party experience, and make sure to arrive early to avoid the queues.

Location: Av. Rafael Puig Lluvina, 5, 38650 Arona, Santa Cruz de Tenerife, Spain
Website: www.facebook.com/envyclubtenerife/

LATE-NIGHT DINING

RESTAURANTE EL CINE

Restaurante El Cine in Los Cristianos is a legendary spot for late-night dining, famous for its simple yet delicious seafood dishes. Known for its lively atmosphere and fast service, the restaurant serves up fresh fish, grilled meats, and the renowned "papas arrugadas" with mojo sauce. Despite its popularity, prices remain reasonable, making it

a great choice for a casual late-night meal.

Tip: Be sure to try their grilled squid or fried octopus, both local favorites.

Location: Location: P.º Juan Bariajo, 8, 38650 Los Cristianos, Santa Cruz de Tenerife, Spain

Website: www.restauranteelcine.com

LA HIERBITA

La Hierbita, housed in a historic building in Santa Cruz, offers a rustic and cozy dining experience. This restaurant is known for its traditional Canarian cuisine, served in a charming antique-filled setting. The menu features hearty dishes perfect for a late-night feast, including stews, grilled meats, and local specialties.

Tip: Try their "ropa vieja" (a traditional stew) or "carne fiesta" (marinated pork) for a taste of authentic Canarian flavors.

Location: C. Clavel, 19, 38003 Santa Cruz de Tenerife, Spain

Website: www.lahierbita.es

RESTAURANTE SAN SEBASTIÁN 57

Situated in Santa Cruz de Tenerife, is renowned for its sophisticated dining and elegant atmosphere. The restaurant specializes in contemporary Mediterranean and Canarian cuisine, offering dishes that are both visually stunning and deliciously crafted. The modern, stylish decor and attentive service make it a popular choice for a refined late-night dining experience.

Tip: The restaurant's tasting menu is a highlight, providing a culinary journey through a variety of exquisite flavors and textures.

Location: Av. de San Sebastián, 57, 38005 Santa Cruz de Tenerife, Spain

Website: www.facebook.com/sansebastian57

RESTAURANTE LA CUPULA

Restaurante La Cupula, located in the five-star Hotel Jardines de Nivaria in Costa Adeje, offers an exquisite fine dining experience. It's known for its fusion of French and Canarian cuisines, presented in an elegant and sophisticated setting. The restaurant, led by the renowned chef Rubén Cabrera, provides a menu that showcases creative and beautifully plated dishes, making it a perfect choice for a classy late-night dining experience.

Tip: Reserve a table by the window for a romantic view. The tasting menu, paired with a selection from their extensive wine cellar, offers a memorable gastronomic journey.

Location: Playa Fañabé, C. París, s/n, 38670 Costa Adeje, Santa Cruz de Tenerife, Spain

Website: www.restaurantelacupula.com

NIGHTLIFE AREAS

VERONICAS STRIP

Veronicas Strip, located in Playa de las Américas, is the epicenter of Tenerife's nightlife. This vibrant area is lined with bars, nightclubs, and music venues, buzzing with energy every night of the week. It's a popular destination for those looking to dance the night away, with a variety of music styles and atmospheres to choose from. The strip attracts a young and lively crowd, making it the perfect place for party-goers.

Tip: Explore different venues to find your preferred music and ambiance, and be prepared for a lively, energetic crowd.

Location: Playa de las Américas, South Tenerife

SAN TELMO (LOS CRISTIANOS)

San Telmo, located in Los Cristianos, offers a more relaxed nightlife experience compared to Veronicas Strip. This area is known for its beautiful sea views, charming terraces, and a variety of bars and restaurants. It's a great place to enjoy a cocktail, live music, and the ocean breeze. San Telmo caters to a more diverse age group and is ideal for those seeking a laid-back evening.

Tip: Enjoy a meal or a drink in one of the terrace bars overlooking the sea, which offer a perfect setting for a romantic or tranquil night out.

Location: Los Cristianos, South Tenerife

LA NORIA STREET (SANTA CRUZ)

La Noria Street in Santa Cruz de Tenerife is known for its vibrant and diverse nightlife. This historic street is lined with a mix of traditional and modern bars, pubs, and restaurants. The area comes alive at night, with locals and tourists mingling in the lively atmosphere. La Noria is perfect for bar-hopping and experiencing the local nightlife scene.

Tip: Visit on a weekend for the liveliest experience, and be sure to try some local tapas as you explore the various establishments.

Location: Located to the south of Plaza Mayor, extending to the Rastro flea market.

Website: www.esmadrid.com/barrios-de-madrid/latina

COSTA ADEJE

The nightlife area in Costa Adeje offers a sophisticated and upscale night out. This area is known for its chic bars, lounges, and clubs, many of which offer live music and entertainment. It's a favorite among couples and groups looking for a more refined evening. The area's elegant establishments, combined with its beautiful setting, make it a perfect choice for a memorable night.

Tip: For a more exclusive experience, visit some of the beachfront clubs, where you can enjoy a cocktail under the stars.

Location: Costa Adeje, South Tenerife

SAFETY TIPS

Exploring Tenerife by night can be an exhilarating experience, but it's important to prioritize your safety to ensure your evening adventures remain pleasant memories. Here are some safety tips to keep in mind:

- **Vigilance is key**: Crowded venues and bustling streets are prime spots for pickpockets. Always be mindful of your personal belongings and consider using anti-theft bags or pouches.
- **Stay in the light**: Stick to well-lit and populated streets, especially if you're venturing out alone. Dark and deserted alleys can be risky, so it's best to avoid them.
- **Trustworthy transport**: Use only reputable taxi companies or verified ride-sharing apps for nighttime travel. It's wise to pre-save the contact details of a reliable taxi service on your phone.
- **Guard your glass**: While enjoying the local nightlife, never leave your drink unattended. Accept beverages only from trusted companions or directly from the bartender.
- **Drink smart**: Consume alcohol in moderation and stay hydrated with water throughout the night. This will help you maintain awareness and make better decisions.
- **Emergency preparedness**: Keep a list of emergency contacts, including local authorities and your embassy, easily accessible. A portable phone charger can be a lifesaver in keeping your device powered up.
- **Document safety**: Carry photocopies of your essential documents, such as your passport, and store the originals in a secure location like a hotel safe.

Remember, the night is yours to enjoy, but staying alert and prepared is the best way to ensure that your nocturnal explorations are safe and enjoyable.

By following these tips and exploring the city by night, you'll be able to experience the magic and charm of the city while staying safe and having an unforgettable time.

ART, HISTORY AND ARCHITECTURE

Tenerife: A Canvas of Nature, History, and Architectural Wonders

Tenerife, the crown jewel of Spain's Canary Islands, is a vibrant tapestry of natural beauty, historical depth, and architectural diversity. Nestled in the Atlantic Ocean, this island is a fusion of breathtaking landscapes and rich cultural heritage, making it a unique destination for art, history, and architecture enthusiasts.

The island's artistic scene is deeply influenced by its diverse cultural roots, ranging from the indigenous Guanche people to Spanish colonial influences. Tenerife's art is a celebration of this blend, visible in its museums and galleries, which showcase everything from ancient artifacts to contemporary works. The TEA Tenerife Espacio de las Artes, for instance, stands as a modern art hub, housing innovative exhibitions and cultural events.

Historically, Tenerife's narrative is as captivating as its landscapes. The island's past is marked by the Guanches, whose mysterious pyramids and cave paintings offer a glimpse into pre-Hispanic life. The Spanish conquest in the 15th century brought a new era, evident in the historic towns like La Laguna, a UNESCO World Heritage Site, known for its well-preserved colonial architecture.

Architecturally, Tenerife is a blend of the old and the new. The island's churches, such as the Candelaria Basilica, showcase exquisite examples of Canarian architecture with their unique Mudejar influences. In contrast, contemporary structures like the Auditorio de Tenerife, designed by Santiago Calatrava, highlight the island's modern architectural prowess.

Tenerife's landscape itself is a masterpiece, dominated by the majestic Mount Teide, Spain's highest peak and a UNESCO World Heritage Site. The surrounding Teide National Park offers a dramatic backdrop, where nature's artistry is on full display.

In essence, Tenerife is not just an island; it's a living museum where every corner tells a story. From its ancient roots to its modern artistic expressions, Tenerife invites visitors to explore a world where history, art, and architecture intertwine in a captivating dance. For those seeking a journey through the vibrant spectrum of cultural and natural beauty, Tenerife offers an unforgettable experience.

ART AND CULTURE IN TENERIFE

AUDITORIO DE TENERIFE-ADÁN MARTÍN

The Auditorio de Tenerife is an architectural masterpiece designed by Santiago Calatrava, resembling a wave in motion. It is a symbol of contemporary architecture and a cultural landmark of the island. The venue hosts a wide range of performances, including opera, classical music concerts, and contemporary shows. The building itself, with its dramatic profile, is a must-see attraction, and attending a performance here is a memorable experience.

Tip: Even if you can't catch a show, consider taking a guided tour of the building to appreciate its unique architecture and learn about its cultural significance.

Location: Av. la Constitución, 1, 38003 Santa Cruz de Tenerife, Spain

Website: www.auditoriodetenerife.com/en/

TEA TENERIFE ESPACIO DE LAS ARTES

TEA Tenerife Espacio de las Artes, also in Santa Cruz, is a modern art complex that combines contemporary art, cinema, and literature. It houses the Óscar Domínguez Institute (a contemporary art museum), a well-stocked public library, and the Cine TEA, which screens independent films. The center regularly hosts art exhibitions, workshops, and cultural events, making it a vibrant hub of Tenerife's contemporary arts scene.

Tip: Visit their temporary exhibitions, which often feature works by local and international contemporary artists.
Location: Av. de San Sebastián, 10, 38003 Santa Cruz de Tenerife, Spain
Website: www.teatenerife.es

CASA DE LOS BALCONES

Casa de los Balcones, located in La Orotava, is a historic house that provides a window into 17th-century Canarian life. The house is famous for its beautiful wooden balconies, a characteristic element of Canarian architecture. Inside, you can explore rooms furnished in the traditional style, a museum of Canarian crafts, and a charming courtyard. The house also has a shop selling local crafts and embroidery.

Tip: Take time to explore the embroidery workshop where you can see artisans at work, keeping traditional techniques alive.
Location: C. San Francisco, 3, 38300 La Orotava, Santa Cruz de Tenerife, Spain
Website: www.casa-balcones.com

MUSEUM OF NATURE AND MAN

The Museo de la Naturaleza y el Hombre is a fascinating museum in Santa Cruz de Tenerife that combines natural sciences and archaeology to provide insight into the natural history and the indigenous Guanche culture of the Canary Islands. The museum houses significant archaeological finds, including mummies and artifacts, and offers interactive exhibits about the islands' volcanic formation, flora, and fauna.

Tip: Don't miss the Guanche mummies, which are some of the most well-preserved examples of indigenous Canarian culture.
Location: C. Fuente Morales, s/n, 38003 Santa Cruz de Tenerife, Spain
Website: www.museosdetenerife.org/muna-museo-de-naturaleza-y-arqueologia/

PIRÁMIDES DE GÜÍMAR

The Pirámides de Güímar are a series of mysterious step pyramids located in the town of Güímar. They were brought to international attention by Norwegian explorer Thor Heyerdahl. The site also features a museum,  a replica of Heyerdahl's boat and botanical gardens showcasing native flora. The complex offers insights into the theories about the origins of the pyramids and their connection with ancient civilizations.

Tip: Visit during the summer solstice to witness the double sunset phenomenon, which aligns with the layout of the pyramids.
Location: C. de Serrano, 122, 28006 Madrid, Spain
Website: www.museolazarogaldiano.es/

MUSEO DE HISTORIA Y ANTROPOLOGÍA DE TENERIFE

The Museo de Historia y Antropología de Tenerife, located in two historic sites – the Casa Lercaro in La Laguna and the Casa de Carta in Valle de Guerra, offers a deep dive into the rich tapestry of Tenerife's history. This museum is a gateway to understanding the island's complex past, from the 15th century to modern times. It provides fascinating insights into the lives of the Guanche people, the original inhabitants of the Canary Islands, and delves into the significant impact of European colonization.

The exhibits thoughtfully display a range of artifacts, from traditional Guanche tools and pottery to items that illustrate the cultural transformations brought about by European influence. The museum not only chronicles historical events but also captures the social and cultural evolution of Tenerife, making it an invaluable resource for both historians and casual visitors.

Tip: To gain a comprehensive understanding, it's recommended to visit both Casa Lercaro and Casa de Carta. Each location has a unique focus, offering different perspectives on Tenerife's historical and cultural journey. The museum frequently hosts temporary exhibitions and cultural events, so check their schedule for any special happenings during your visit.

Location: C. San Agustín, 22, 38201 La Laguna, Santa Cruz de Tenerife, Spain

Website: www.museosdetenerife.org/mha-museo-de-historia-y-antropologia/

HISTORICAL AND ARCHITECTURAL LANDMARKS IN TENERIFE

BASILICA OF CANDELARIA

The Basilica of Candelaria is a significant religious and historical landmark located in the town of Candelaria. It is home to the statue of the Virgin of Candelaria, the patron saint of the Canary Islands. The basilica, with its impressive architecture, is a pilgrimage site and holds great cultural importance. The surrounding square and the statues of the Guanche kings add to the historical significance of the site.

Tip: Explore the town of Candelaria to experience its religious and cultural heritage, and visit the nearby beach for its black sand and sea views.

Location: Pl. Patrona de Canarias, 1, 38530 Candelaria, Santa Cruz de Tenerife, Spain
Website: www.candelaria.es/basilica-nuestra-senora-de-candelaria/

CASTILLO DE SAN MIGUEL

The Castillo de San Miguel is an important historical fortress located in Garachico. This 16th-century castle was built as a defense against pirate attacks and now serves as a cultural center and museum. The castle offers insights into the history of the island and its defense systems. Visitors can enjoy panoramic views of the coast from the top of the castle.

Tip: Visit the exhibition inside the castle to learn about the history of Garachico and the role of the fortress in protecting the town.
Location: 38450 Garachico, Santa Cruz de Tenerife, Spain
Website: http://www.turismo.garachico.es/index.php?option=com_recursos&task=mostrarrecurso&id_recurso=70&Itemid=28

IGLESIA DE LA CONCEPCIÓN

The Iglesia de la Concepción is a beautiful church located in the historic center of La Laguna. This church, dating back to the 16th century, is an excellent example of Canarian religious architecture, featuring a striking Mudejar ceiling, a beautiful baroque façade, and an iconic bell tower. The church has been a central part of La Laguna's religious and social life for centuries.

Tip: Climb the church's bell tower for a breathtaking view of the city and its surroundings.
Location: Pl. de la Concepción, 10, 38201 La Laguna, Santa Cruz de Tenerife, Spain
Website: www.turismo.aytolalaguna.es/iglesia-de-nuestra-senora-de-la-concepcion/

CASA DE LA ADUANA TENERIFE

The Casa de la Aduana, or the Customs House, is a historically significant building located in Puerto de la Cruz. Dating back to the 17th century, it served as the main customs office for the port. The building is an excellent example of traditional Canarian architecture, with its wooden balconies and typical courtyard. Today, it hosts cultural events and exhibitions, making it a point of interest for those exploring the history of Tenerife.

Tip: While exploring the building, take a walk around the old town of Puerto de la Cruz to see more traditional architecture and experience the town's historic charm.

Location: Pl. de Europa, 2, 38400 Puerto de la Cruz, Santa Cruz de Tenerife, Spain
Website: www.webtenerife.co.uk/tenerife/the-island/municipalities/puerto-cruz/places-interest/casa-real-aduana/

CONVENTO DE SAN FRANCISCO

The Convento de San Francisco, located in Garachico, is one of the oldest convents in Tenerife. The convent features a mix of architectural styles, including Mudejar, Gothic, and Baroque elements. The building has survived volcanic eruptions and pirate attacks, and today, it houses the San Francisco Convent Art Centre, showcasing art and historical exhibits. The serene courtyard and well-preserved architecture make it a tranquil and enlightening place to visit.

Tip: Check out the exhibition schedule to catch art displays or historical exhibits during your visit.

Location: Gta. San Francisco, 1, 38450 Garachico, Santa Cruz de Tenerife, Spain
Website: www.webtenerife.co.uk/tenerife/the-island/municipalities/laguna/places-interest/cristo-de-la-laguna

CASA DE LOS CAPITANES GENERALES

The Casa de los Capitanes Generales, nestled in the heart of La Laguna's historic center – a UNESCO World Heritage Site – is an architectural gem and a significant landmark in Tenerife's history. Built in the 17th century, this historic building exudes the charm of traditional Canarian architecture, most notably through its stunning facade and intricate wooden balconies. Originally serving as the residence of the military governors of Tenerife, the building has been a silent witness to various historical events shaping the island.

Today, the Casa de los Capitanes Generales has transformed into a vibrant cultural center, enriching La Laguna's cultural scene. It hosts a variety of cultural activities, exhibitions, and events, making it a focal point for both locals and tourists interested in the arts and history. The interior of the building is as impressive as its exterior, with well-preserved rooms and halls that showcase the lifestyle and customs of its former inhabitants.

.Tip: After visiting the Casa, take the time to explore the surrounding streets of La Laguna's historic center. The area is rich in beautifully preserved buildings and offers a journey through the architectural evolution and history of the Canary Islands. Keep an eye out for temporary exhibitions in the Casa that often highlight local artists and historical themes.

Location: C. Obispo Rey Redondo, 5, 38201 La Laguna, Santa Cruz de Tenerife, Spain
Website: www.turismo.aytolalaguna.es/en/casa-de-los-capitanes-generales/

DAY TRIPS FROM TENERIFE

LA GOMERA

A day trip to La Gomera offers a chance to explore an unspoiled and diverse island, just a short ferry ride from Tenerife. Known for its lush green landscapes, ancient laurel forests, and traditional whistling language (Silbo Gomero), La Gomera is a UNESCO Biosphere Reserve. Highlights include Garajonay National Park, the quaint capital of San Sebastián, and stunning viewpoints like Mirador de Abrante. **Tip**: Consider taking a guided tour to see the island's highlights and learn about its unique culture and ecology. **Location**: La Gomera, Santa Cruz de Tenerife, Spain; Travel Time: Approximately 50 minutes by ferry from Los Cristianos.
Website: www.spain.info/en/region/la-gomera-island/

EL HIERRO

El Hierro, the smallest and westernmost of the Canary Islands, is a hidden gem known for its dramatic landscapes and ecological diversity. The island offers a tranquil escape with its volcanic terrain, pine forests, and coastal cliffs. Key attractions include the El Sabinar juniper trees natural swimming pools at La Maceta, and the Faro de Orchilla lighthouse.

Tip: Rent a car to explore the island at your own pace, as public transportation options are limited.
Location: El Hierro, Santa Cruz de Tenerife, Spain; Travel Time: Around 2.5 hours by ferry from Los Cristianos
Website: www.spain.info/en/region/el-hierro-island/

LA PALMA

La Palma, often referred to as 'La Isla Bonita' (The Beautiful Island), is known for its lush vegetation, rugged volcanic landscapes, and clear night skies. Highlights include the Caldera de Taburiente National Park, the Roque de los Muchachos Observatory, and charming towns like Santa Cruz de La Palma. The island's network of hiking trails offers stunning views and varied terrain.

Tip: Tip: Hiking in Caldera de Taburiente National Park is a must-do; wear appropriate footwear and bring plenty of water.

Location: La Palma, Santa Cruz de Tenerife, Spain; Travel Time: Around 2.5 hours by ferry from Los Cristianos

Website: www.spain.info/en/region/la-palma-island/

GRAN CANARIA

A trip to Gran Canaria, Tenerife's neighboring island, provides a contrast with its diverse landscapes, ranging from sandy beaches to dunes and green valleys. Key attractions include the Maspalomas Dunes, the picturesque village of Teror, and the capital city of Las Palmas. Gran Canaria also offers vibrant cultural experiences and bustling markets.

Tip: Visit the historic quarter of Vegueta in Las Palmas for a walk through history and culture.

Location: Gran Canaria, Las Palmas, Spain; Travel Time: Around 1.5 to 2.5 hours by ferry from Santa Cruz de Tenerife

Website: www.spain.info/en/region/gran-canaria-island/

LOS CRISTIANOS

Although not an island, the town of Los Cristianos in Tenerife itself is worth a day trip. Once a humble fishing village, it's now a lively resort town with beautiful beaches, a variety of restaurants, and a bustling harbor offering boat trips and water sports. The town retains some of its original charm and is a great place for shopping, dining, and relaxing by the sea.

Tip: Take a boat trip from Los Cristianos harbor to spot dolphins and whales in their natural habitat.

Location: Los Cristianos, Santa Cruz de Tenerife, Spain; Travel Time: Easily accessible from anywhere in South Tenerife
Website: www.hellocanaryislands.com/tourist-resorts/tenerife/los-cristianos/

CALLAO SALVAJE

Callao Salvaje is a tranquil resort town located on Tenerife's west coast. Known for its peaceful ambiance, it's a great escape from the more bustling tourist areas. The town has a small but lovely beach, Playa de Ajabo, and is surrounded by natural beauty, making it ideal for relaxation. There are several cafes and restaurants where you can enjoy local and international cuisine.

Tip: Visit the local beach for a swim and sunbathe, and explore the town's laid-back atmosphere.

Location: Costa Adeje, Santa Cruz de Tenerife, Spain; Travel Time: A short drive from major resorts in South Tenerife
Website: www.hellocanaryislands.com/tourist-resorts/tenerife/costa-adeje/

PLAYA LA ARENA

Playa La Arena is a beautiful black sand beach located in the resort town of Puerto de Santiago. It's known for its stunning natural beauty, crystal-clear waters, and the dramatic cliffs of Los Gigantes in the background. The beach is well-maintained, with amenities like sun loungers, showers, and lifeguards, making it ideal for a relaxing day trip. The town also offers a variety of dining options and shops.

Tip: Stay until sunset to witness the spectacular views against the backdrop of the cliffs.

Location: Playa de la Arena, Santa Cruz de Tenerife, Spain; Travel Time: Easily accessible from major tourist areas in South Tenerife

Website: www.hellocanaryislands.com/beaches/tenerife/playa-de-la-arena-0/

PUERTO DE LA CRUZ

Puerto de la Cruz, in the north of Tenerife, offers a blend of traditional Canarian charm and modern tourist amenities. The town is known for its historical buildings, beautiful gardens, and the famous Lago Martiánez pool complex. Other attractions include the Botanical Garden and the vibrant Plaza del Charco. Puerto de la Cruz also offers a variety of shops, cafes, and restaurants.

Tip: Don't miss a visit to Loro Parque, one of the world's most renowned renowned animal parks, located just outside the town.

Location: Puerto de la Cruz, Santa Cruz de Tenerife, Spain; Travel Time: Approximately 1 hour by car from South Tenerife

Website: www.spain.info/en/destination/puerto-la-cruz/

COASTAL WALKS

Tenerife offers numerous coastal walks that showcase the island's stunning shoreline. These walks vary in difficulty and length, providing breathtaking views of the sea, cliffs, and natural beaches. Popular routes include the walk from Playa de las Américas to La Caleta and the coastal path in Los Gigantes.

Tip: Wear comfortable shoes and bring sunscreen and water, especially on sunny days.
Location: Depends on the starting point; many coastal walks are easily accessible from major tourist areas.
Website: www.alltrails.com/spain/tenerife/walking (login or account needed) or www.walkingtenerife.co.uk

HIKING TRAILS

Tenerife is a hiker's paradise, with trails that traverse diverse landscapes, from the lunar-like terrain of Teide National Park to the lush laurel forests of Anaga Rural Park. Popular hikes include the Masca Gorge, the trails around Roques de Garcia, and the paths in Teno Rural Park. These hikes offer a chance to experience the island's natural beauty up close.

Tip: Check the difficulty level and distance of the trails beforehand and always hike with appropriate gear, including sturdy shoes and adequate water.

Location: Varies depending on the trail location
Website: www.webtenerife.co.uk/what-to-do/nature/hiking/ or www.alltrails.com/spain/tenerife (login or account needed)

END NOTE

As we draw the final lines of this Tenerife guide, it becomes clear that Tenerife is much more than a destination; it is a mosaic of natural beauty, rich history, and vibrant culture. This island, the largest of the Canary archipelago, invites you to explore its diverse landscapes, from the majestic peaks of Teide National Park to the serene beaches along its coastline. Tenerife is a symphony of experiences, a place where every volcanic rock tells a tale, and every ocean wave sings a lullaby of tranquility.

The story of Tenerife is woven from the threads of its past and the vibrancy of its present. The ancient paths of the Guanche echo with the footsteps of history, while the lively streets of Santa Cruz buzz with contemporary energy. The island's architecture, a blend of traditional Canarian and modern styles, mirrors Tenerife's ability to respect its roots while evolving with time.

Tenerife's culinary landscape is as varied as its ecosystems. From the rustic guachinches serving traditional fare to the sophisticated restaurants offering innovative dishes, the island delights the palate. Its cuisine is a celebration of flavors, a testament to the island's rich agricultural bounty and its love for the sea.

Departing from Tenerife, you carry with you more than just memories; you take a piece of its soul. The aroma of pine forests, the warmth of the Canarian sun, the taste of papas arrugadas, and the grandeur of its natural wonders linger with you. You leave behind the charming villages, the dramatic cliffs, and the vibrant fiestas, but you are comforted by the knowledge that Tenerife is a place to return to.

Tenerife is a testament to the spirit and warmth of its inhabitants. It's an island that celebrates life and resilience, a place where nature's majesty and human creativity live in harmony. Tenerife is a destination for all, an island that reveals its mysteries and familiar joys with each visit.

As this guide concludes, remember that Tenerife is not just a journey's end; it's a continuing adventure. It's an island that stays with you, inviting you to return, to explore, and to fall in love with it again and again. Tenerife awaits your next visit with open arms and a promise: the enchantment of this island paradise is everlasting, and each return will be as captivating as the first.

Embark on an exploration of this island gem, and let the enduring charm of Tenerife inspire you, today and forever.

EXTRARA RESOURCES

Tenerife maps

Tenerife Tourist Map

Tenerife Road Map

Tenerife Bus Map

Tenerife Resorts and Beaches

Tenerife Island Map

San Cristobal and Santa cruz Map

Canary Islands Tourism Consortium

Tenerife Tourist Offices

TRAVEL

PLACES TO SEE:

LOCAL FOOD TO TRY:

| DAY 1 | DAY 2 | DAY 3 |

| DAY 4 | DAY 5 | DAY 6 |

NOTES

PLANNER

Loved Your Journey With Our Guide? 🌟
Your feedback makes a world of difference! If our guide helped you explore or enjoy your destination, we would be thrilled if you could take a moment to leave us a 5-star review on our product page.🙏

Simply click the link or go to any of our product pages on your preferred retailer website and **share your recommendations.**
https://www.amazon.com/stores/Tailored-Travel-Guides/author/B0C4TV5TZX

Scan the QR Code to share your recommendations

Join our Tailored Travel Guides Network
for more benefits by accessing this link:
https://mailchi.mp/d151cba349e8/ttgnetwork
Or by scanning the QR code

Thank you for chosing Tailored Travel Guides!

Discover your journey!

UNLOCK A WORLD OF UNFORGETTABLE EXPERIENCES WITH TAILORED TRAVEL GUIDES!

Unlock a world of unforgettable experiences with Tailored Travel Guides! As your go-to source for personalized and meticulously crafted travel guides, we ensure that every adventure is uniquely yours. Our team of dedicated travel experts and local insiders design each guide with your preferences, interests, and travel style in mind, providing you with the ultimate customized travel experience.

Embark on your next journey with confidence, knowing that Tailored Travel Guides has got you covered. To explore more exceptional destinations and discover a treasure trove of additional guides, visit www.tailoredtravelguides.com. or our collection available on:

Amazon at this link: www.amazon.com/stores/Tailored-Travel-Guides/author/B0C4TV5TZX or
on **Google Play**, at this link: https://play.google.com/store/books/author?id=Tailored+Travel+Guides
on **Etsy**, at this link: https://tailoredtravelguides.etsy.com

Happy travels, and here's to a lifetime of remarkable memories!

ALSO IN THE SERIES

Malaga

Barcelona

Valencia

Seville

Cordoba

Bilbao

Toledo

San Sebastian

Madrid

Tenerife

Granada

CHECK OUT THE ITALY UNCOVERED SERIES

Turin

Bologna

Rome

Milan

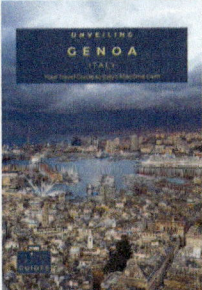 
Genoa

Venice

Verona

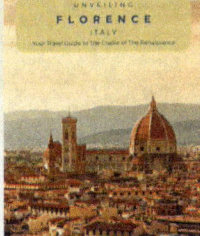 
Florence

Naples

Palermo

CHECK OUT THE FRANCE UNVEILED SERIES

  **Marseille**

  **Nantes**

  **Toulouse**

  **Nice**

  **Paris**

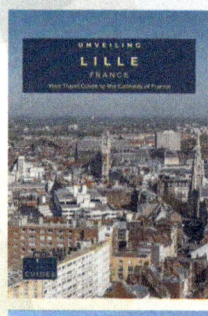  **Lille**

  **Lyon**

  **Montpellier**

  **Bordeaux**

  **Strasbourg**

Printed in Great Britain
by Amazon